AF447243

Extremely Funny
WOULD YOU RATHER
GAME
TURN BACK RIGHT NOW IF
YOUR SQUEAMISH OR
EASILY OFFENDED
ROFL
ADULTS ONLY EDITION

S.N PUBLISHERS

This
Would You Rather
Book Belongs To

____

WOULD YOU RATHER

Fart an extremely
smelly fart loudly
everytime you say
hello
OR
Have breath that
smells like your
farts?

WOULD YOU RATHER

Chicken feet for
your hands
OR
Fart a chicken
egg everytime
you smile?

WOULD YOU RATHER

Ride a Bull

OR

Ride a Shark?

WOULD YOU RATHER

A fart sound
laugh
OR
Shit yourself
in public
everytime
you laugh?

WOULD YOU RATHER

Wake up naked at
mums house with
all your family there,
but not know how
you got there
OR
Waking up naked at
the shopping center
everyday for the
next year?

WOULD YOU RATHER

Sex with an ugly
person with the
light on
OR
Super hot sex
with the light off
but not know
who it is?

WOULD YOU RATHER

Wake up naked
with your
partners sister
OR
Your partner
waking up
naked with
your sisters?

WOULD YOU RATHER

Ride a shark
naked at the
public zoo
OR
Watch your
partner do
it?

WOULD YOU RATHER

Sex with your
partner in your
local shopping
centre
OR
Sex in front or
your partners
mum and dad?

WOULD YOU RATHER

Mum catches
you watching
porn
OR
You catching
your mum
watching
porn?

WOULD YOU RATHER

Slap mum in
the face
OR
Kick the
famliy dog?

WOULD YOU RATHER

Eat five live
spiders
OR
Sleep with 10
snakes in your
bed for the
night?

WOULD YOU RATHER

Eat cat shit

OR

Eat your

own shit?

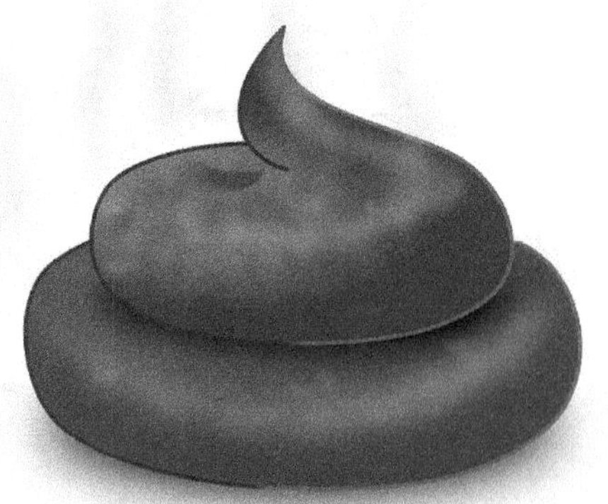

WOULD YOU RATHER

Bite the
family dog
OR
Let 3 family
members
bite your
hand?

WOULD YOU RATHER

Save your

partner

OR

Save

yourself?

WOULD YOU RATHER

Win a millon
OR
Win your true
love?

WOULD YOU RATHER

Win 5 million
OR
Have your lover win 10 million, but he/she may dump your arse?

WOULD YOU RATHER

Have sex with
your partners
mum and dad
OR
Sex with your
partner in front
of your mum
and dad?

WOULD YOU RATHER

Needle in
the eye
OR
Needle
under your
big toe nail?

WOULD YOU RATHER

Trapped in an elevator with your ex's brother
OR
Trap with your ex one last time?

WOULD YOU RATHER

Stub your toe 10 times a day

OR

Run across lego glued to the floor?

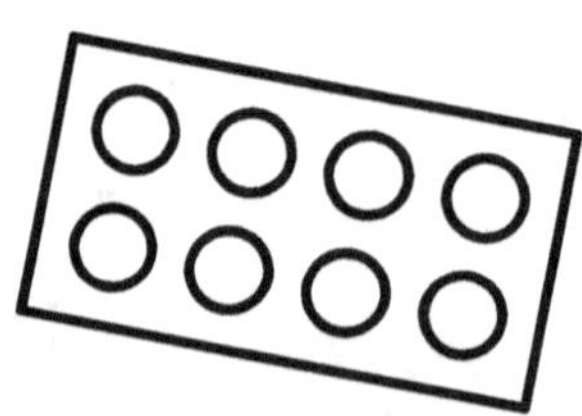

WOULD YOU RATHER

Tongue punch your lovers fart box
OR
Your lover tongue punch your fart box?

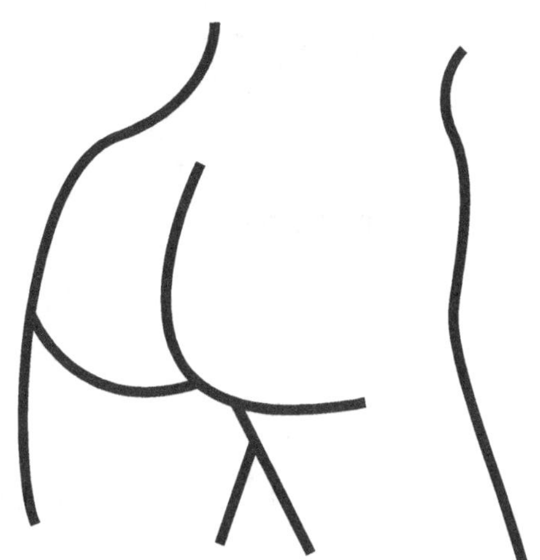

WOULD YOU RATHER

Sex with a sexy
hot alien
OR
Sex with a super
hot sexy zombie?

WOULD YOU RATHER

Be able to

see your

future

OR

See your

partners

past?

WOULD YOU RATHER

Randomly Laugh aloud in public
OR
Randomly shout in public?

WOULD YOU RATHER

Give yourself
a blowjob
OR
Fuck your
own arse?

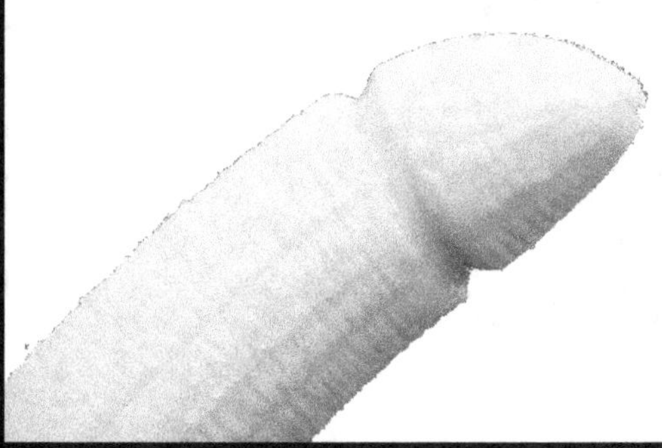

WOULD YOU RATHER

Lick your own vag

OR

Sit your arse on a cucumber?

Would You Rather

Fuck me right now
OR
That ugly twat
over there?

Point to another
player in the game

WOULD YOU RATHER

Suck on a hairy smelly old mans armpits
OR
Suck on nan's yellowing rotten smelly big toe?

WOULD YOU RATHER

Have huge
nipples for
fingers
OR
Huge
fingers for
nipples?

WOULD YOU RATHER

Catch your parents in a porn film

OR

Catch your partner in the a porn film?

Clamp's on
your nipples
OR
Hammer on
your baby
toe's?

WOULD YOU RATHER

Tear off your

clothes in a

night club

OR

Have

someone else

tear them off

for you?

Would You Rather

Know what
your dog is
thinking
OR
Be able to talk
to your dog and
let everyone
else think your
crazy?

WOULD YOU RATHER

Eat a whole tub
of butter with 3
fresh garlic
cloves
OR
Mix a jar of
peanutbutter &
mayonnaise
and eat that all?

WOULD YOU RATHER

Eat a jar of jam
that taste like
dog shit
OR
Have it
massaged all
over your body?

WOULD YOU RATHER

Shit yourself
while standing
at the altar
OR
Puke on the
new wife
wedding
dress?

WOULD YOU RATHER

Naked pole dance in front of your grandparents
OR
Made to watch them pole dance naked?

WOULD YOU RATHER

Sneeze shit
everytime you
Sneeze
OR
Shit handfuls
of snot
everytime you
take a shit?

WOULD YOU RATHER

Have hot steamy
sex with a rotten
sexy zombie
OR
Dangerous sex with
a blood firsty
vampire?

WOULD YOU RATHER

Sex with an alien who has a 3-headed 8" long Tongue
OR
Sex with a ghost who has an extra thick 16" long penis?

WOULD YOU RATHER

Wake up as a woman trapped in a mans body
OR
Wake up as man Trapped in a womans body?

WOULD YOU RATHER

Get told by

your partner

their gay

OR

Get told by

your partner

they just

cheated on

you?

WOULD YOU RATHER

Turn into the opposite
sex for a day
OR
Turn into an animal
for a week?

WOULD YOU RATHER

A nose that
looked like a
penis
OR
A mouth that
looked like a
hairy Vagina?

WOULD YOU RATHER

Drink a
diarrhea
milkshake
or
Have smelly
breath like
bad
diarrhea?

WOULD YOU RATHER

Suck on a
huge dick
with old dried
come on it
OR
Suck on a
huge sweaty
hairy smelly
vagina?

WOULD YOU RATHER

Get anal
fucked by a
horse
OR
Give the
same horse
a blowjob?

WOULD YOU RATHER

Eat a pint class full of a strangers pubic hair
OR
Drink a pint of your grandads piss?

WOULD YOU RATHER

Your wife see's
you sitting in a
gay bar
or
Your wifes
parents see you
sitting a gay bar
and tells your
partner about it?

WOULD YOU RATHER

Drop your phone in
a public toilet
covered in someone
else's poo and have
to fish it out yourself
OR
Pretent it's your
partners phone and
make them fish it
out?

WOULD YOU RATHER

Own a dragon

OR

Be a gay

dragon?

Would You Rather

Have an elephants
trunk for your nose
OR
Have tiny elephant
ball on your chin?

WOULD YOU RATHER

Be

immortal

OR

Be able to

travel

through

time?

WOULD YOU RATHER

Wear your
nans 3 day
old knickers
for the day
OR
Wear her
teeth for a
week?

WOULD YOU RATHER

Marry an ugly
rich person
who treats
you like a
super star
OR
Be a superstar
for just a day?

WOULD YOU RATHER

Your wife/husband
be able to read
your mind once a
month
OR
Your
wife/husbands
parents read your
mind once a week?

WOULD YOU RATHER

Mustard in

your eye

OR

Drink a pint

of mustard?

WOULD YOU RATHER

Have a huge oversized long tongue you can not fit in your mouth

OR

Have a 3" penis as your nose?

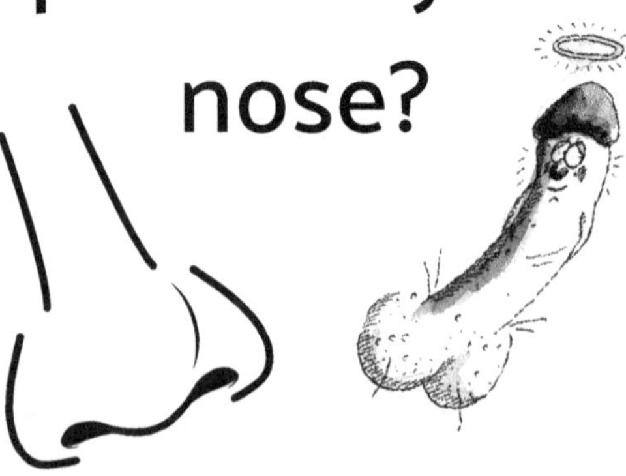

WOULD YOU RATHER

Massage in
dog poo
OR
Massage in
mud with
hundred of
unknow bugs
in it?

WOULD YOU RATHER

Shave your
partners
eyebrows
OR
Shave your
partner head
bald?

WOULD YOU RATHER

Be trapped in an
elevator with
your significant
other for a day
OR
Be trapped with
your ex lover for
2 days?

WOULD YOU RATHER

Ditch the
wife/husband for
a stripper club
night
OR
Be the stripper at
the club the
wife/husband
ditched you for?

WOULD YOU RATHER

Long hairs

growing out

from your nose

OR

A huge Spot

right on the

centre of your

chin?

WOULD YOU RATHER

Eat the families
pet gold fish
and pretent it
died
OR
Cook the pet
dog and
pretent it's
chicken?

WOULD YOU RATHER

Suck on your 2
day old
pants/Knickers
OR
Lick and taste
your week old
dirty smelly
socks?

WOULD YOU RATHER

Eat a cockroach
OR
Drink a pint of sweat?

WOULD YOU RATHER

Lose all of your teeth

OR

Lose all of your hair?

WOULD YOU RATHER

Eat a 3 day

old dead cat

OR

Drink a

bucket full of

gabbage juice

form your

bins?

WOULD YOU RATHER

100 bugs in
your
pants/Knickers
or
1000 bugs in
your hair?

WOULD YOU RATHER

Have 10 spiders
run over your
body
OR
500
cockroaches
running up
your legs?

WOULD YOU RATHER

Drink a
month old
cockroach
milkshake
OR
Eat 50 Live
cockroaches?

WOULD YOU RATHER

Go a year
without
sex
OR
Go a year
without
money?

WOULD YOU RATHER

Be 100% grumpy for the rest of your life
OR
100% happy just once a month?

WOULD YOU RATHER

Accidentally like your ex's new profile picture for the world to see on facebook

OR

Your new partner publicly sharing 10 naked pictures of you on facebook for the world to see?

WOULD YOU RATHER

Be forced to
sing at work
everyday at the
top of your
voice
OR
Be naked at
work everyday?

WOULD YOU RATHER

One more
time with
hot ex
girlfriend/boyfriend
OR
Your new
partner win 10
million?

WOULD YOU RATHER

Travel 25 years
into your future
OR
Travel 10 years
into your
partners past
before you new
them?

WOULD YOU RATHER

Have a bee

sting on your

bum

OR

A snake bite

your face?

WOULD YOU RATHER

An elephant stand
on your foot
OR
Fall face first into
elephants shit?

WOULD YOU RATHER

Eat cow
shit
OR
Drink fresh
cow's piss
as it's
pissing?

WOULD YOU RATHER

Get a bite
on your toe
by a poison
spider
OR
Get a snake
bite on your
top lip?

WOULD YOU RATHER

Sit on a

chair or

razors

OR

Sit on a

chair of

needles?

WOULD YOU RATHER

Watch porn

by yourself

OR

Watch porn

with your ex

partner?

Walk across

a path of

lego

OR

Walk across

a path of

class?

WOULD YOU RATHER

Go to your

school reunion

a rich

somebody who

no one likes

OR

Go back still as

the school

joker?

WOULD YOU RATHER

Burn all dogs
and one cat
OR
Burn all
house cats
and one dog?

WOULD YOU RATHER

All your dirty

sexy secrets

shared in

public
OR
Shared to all

your work

mates?

WOULD YOU RATHER

Wake up
naked next
to your step
sister
OR
Wake up to
your naked
step sister?

WOULD YOU RATHER

Get sexual

punishment

OR

Give sexual

punishment?

WOULD YOU RATHER

Be getting
whipped
OR
Be getting
chained up?

WOULD YOU RATHER

Catch your
mum cheating
on dad
OR
Catch your
partner
cheating on
you?

WOULD YOU RATHER

Catch your
mum and dad
having anal sex
OR
Watch your
nan sucking on
grandads old
penis?

WOULD YOU RATHER

Eat a live toad

OR

Eat a dead frog?

WOULD YOU RATHER

Fake your partners death
OR
Have sex 3 times with your partners mum/dad?

WOULD YOU RATHER

Die right

now

OR

Take your

chances in

prison for

the next 15

years?

WOULD YOU RATHER

Take your Mrs/husband to a fancy dinner

OR

Take your ex to the movies one last time?

WOULD YOU RATHER

40 days

without sex

OR

60 days

without your

partner?

WOULD YOU RATHER

Make out with
your partners
mum
OR
Make out with
your partner
dad?

www.ingramcontent.com/pod-product-compliance
Lightning Source LLC
Chambersburg PA
CBHW071451130726
47997CB00006B/2321